# **Bloke**jokes **2**

Edited by
**Louise Johnson**

**CARLTON**
BOOKS

THIS IS A CARLTON BOOK

This edition published by
Carlton Books Limited 2005
20 Mortimer Street
London W1T 3JW

ISBN 1 84442 361 1

Printed and bound in Singapore

Why is it difficult to find blokes who are **sensitive, caring** and **good looking**?

They have boyfriends already.

**Why** is a computer like a **penis**?

If you don't apply the appropriate protective measures, it can spread viruses.

# Why do blokes like **masturbation**?

Because it's sex with someone they love.

Why did the man **cross** the **road**?

He heard the chicken was a slut.

# Why don't women **blink** during **foreplay**?

They don't have time.

Why do black widow spiders **kill** their males after **mating**?

To stop the snoring before it starts.

Why is **sleeping** with a bloke like watching a **soap opera**?

Just when it's getting interesting they're finished until next time.

Why do blokes have a **penis** and a **brain**?

No one knows – there isn't enough blood to supply both at the same time.

Why should you never
let your bloke's
**mind wander**?

Because it's too little to be
let out alone.

Why do blokes find it **difficult** to make **eye contact**?

Breasts don't have eyes.

Why will a woman rarely **make a fool** of a man?

Most of them are the do-it-yourself types.

# Why go for **younger** men?

You might as well – they never mature anyway.

Why should you **never worry** about doing **housework**?

No man ever made love to a woman because the house was spotless.

Why do blokes **name** their **penises**?

Because they don't trust a stranger with 90% of their decisions.

Why are all dumb **blonde** jokes **one-liners**?

So blokes can remember them.

Why is a bloke's **penis** like a **Rubik's cube**?

The more you play with it the harder it gets.

# Why is it **good** that there are **women** astronauts?

So that when the crew get lost in space, at least the women will ask for directions.

Why **don't** blokes often show their **true feelings**?

Because they don't have feelings.

# Why would women be **better off** if blokes treated them like **cars**?

At least then they would get a little attention every 6 months or 5,000 miles, whichever came first.

Why do doctors **slap** babies' **bums** right after they're **born**?

To knock the penises off the clever ones.

# Why is **food** better than **men**?

Because you don't have to wait an hour for seconds.

Why do blokes like **BMWs**?

They can spell it.

?

Why do blokes have their **best ideas** during sex?

Because they're plugged into a genius.

# Why do blokes always **look stupid**?

Because they are stupid.

Why did the man **cross** the **road**?

Never mind that! What's he doing out of the kitchen?

Why is **psychoanalysis** quicker for **blokes** than for **women**?

When it's time to go back to childhood, they're already there.

Why do only **10%** of blokes go to **heaven**?

Because if there were any more it would be hell.

# Why do blokes **hate** wearing **condoms**?

Because it cuts off the circulation to their brains.

# Why can't blokes make **pancakes**?

Because they're useless tossers.

## Why do women **rub** their **eyes** when they wake up?

Because they don't have balls to scratch.

Why is **wee** yellow and **sperm** white?

So a bloke can tell if he's coming or going.

# Why shouldn't you **chain** a bloke to the **sink**?

He won't be able to reach the ironing.

# Why do women **fake orgasms**?

Because blokes fake foreplay.

# Why do blokes go **bald**?

To stop them having any more crap hair cuts!

## Why do blokes buy **electric lawnmowers**?

So they can find their way back to the house.

Why don't blokes use **toilet paper**?

Because God made them perfect asses.

What's the difference between a **bloke** and a **pig**?

A pig doesn't turn into a bloke after two pints of lager!

What's the difference
between **hard** and **dark**?

It stays dark all night.

What's the difference between a **bloke** and a **shopping trolley**?

Sometimes a shopping trolley has a mind of its own.

What's the difference between a **bloke** and **childbirth**?

One can be terribly painful and sometimes almost unbearable while the other is only having a baby.

What's the difference between a **bloke** and a **bloke's photo**?

The photo is fully developed.

What's the difference between a **bar** and a **clitoris**?

Most blokes have no trouble finding a bar.

What's the difference between a **bloke** and a **computer**?

You only have to punch the information into a computer once.

What's the difference between an **attractive man** and an **ugly man**?

About 10 glasses of wine.

What's the difference between your **husband** and your **lover**?

About four hours.

# What's the difference between **light** and **hard**?

A bloke can sleep with a light on.

What's the difference
between a **bloke** and
a **piece of cheese**?

Cheese matures.

?

What's the difference between a **golf ball** and a **G-spot**?

Men will always look for a golf ball.

# What's the difference between **single** women and **married** women?

Single women go home, see what's in the fridge, then go to bed. Married women go home, see what's in the bed, then go to the fridge!

What's the difference
between a **porcupine**
and a **sports car**?

A porcupine has pricks on
the outside.

What's the difference between a **bloke** and a **battery**?

A battery has a positive side!

What's the difference between a single 40-year-old **woman** and a single 40-year-old **bloke**?

The 40-year-old woman often thinks of having children and the 40-year-old bloke often thinks about dating them.

What's the difference between a **new husband** and a **new dog**?

After a year, the dog is still excited to see you.

# What do you call a **handcuffed** bloke?

Trustworthy.

What do you call a bloke with **90%** of his intelligence **gone**?

Divorced.

What do you call a woman who does the **same amount** of **work** as a bloke?

A lazy cow.

What do you call a bloke
with **half a brain**?

Gifted.

What do you call 200 blokes at the **bottom** of the **sea**?

A good start.

What do you call a woman who knows where her husband is **every night**?

A widow.

What do you call a bloke with **99%** of his brain **missing**?

Castrated.

What do you call **144 blokes** in a room?

Gross stupidity.

What do you call **12 naked blokes** sitting on each other's **shoulders**?

A scrotum pole.

What do you call a woman **without** an **arse**?

Single.

What do you call that **useless** flap of skin on the end of a **penis**?

A bloke!

What do you call a **musician** without a **girlfriend**?

Homeless.

# How do we know **God** is a **man**?

Because if God were a woman, sperm would taste like chocolate.

Why did **God** make man **before** woman?

You need a rough draft before you make the final copy.

Why was **Moses** wandering through the desert for **40 years**?

Because blokes refuse to ask for directions!

What did God say after **creating man**?

I must be able to do better
than that.

Why did God put **blokes on Earth**?

Because a vibrator can't mow the lawn.

What do you instantly
know about a
**well-dressed bloke**?

His wife is good at picking
out clothes.

What do **electric trains** and **breasts** have **in common**?

They're intended for children but it's blokes who usually end up playing with them.

What **part** of a bloke **grows** the more you **stroke it**?

His ego.

# What do blokes consider **house cleaning**?

Lifting their feet so you can vacuum under them.

What have you got if you have **100 blokes** buried up to their necks in **sand**?

Not enough sand.

What's a bloke's idea of a
**romantic** evening out?

A candlelit football stadium.

## What are a **woman's** four favourite **animals**?

A mink in the wardrobe,
a Jaguar in the garage,
a tiger in the bedroom and
an ass who'll pay for it all.

What do you have when you have **two little balls** in your **hand**?

A bloke's undivided attention.

What's the **best way** to get a bloke to **do something**?

Suggest he's too old for it.

What is the one thing that all blokes at **singles bars** have **in common**?

They're married.

# What should you do if your bloke **walks out**?

Shut the door after him.

## What is a bloke's view of **safe sex**?

A padded headboard.

What's the only time a bloke thinks about a **candlelit dinner**?

When the power goes off.

What's the **definition** of a **bachelor**?

A bloke who's missed the opportunity to make a woman miserable.

## What's a bloke's idea of **foreplay**?

Half an hour of begging.

# What's the **best time** to try to **change** a man?

When he's in nappies.

## What are the **measurements** of the **perfect husband**?

82-20-45. That's 82 years old, £20 million in the bank and a 45-degree fever.

What's a world **without blokes**?

A world full of fat, happy women.

What does a bloke consider a **seven-course meal**?

A hot dog and a six-pack of beer.

What do **fat blokes** and **mopeds** have in common?

They're both a good ride, but you'd die if your mates saw you on one.

What does the **smart** bloke do in an **M&M factory**?

Proofread.

What does a bloke have to do to keep you **interested** in **his company**?

Own it!

# What does a girl have to **say** to **seduce** a bloke?

'Hi.'

# Why are **blokes** like **floor tiles**?

Lay them right the first time and you can walk all over them for the rest of your life.

# Why are **boring blokes** like **snot**?

They get up your nose.

# Why are **blokes** like **cool bags**?

Load them with beer and you can take them anywhere.

Why are **blokes** like **high heels**?

They're easy to walk on once you get the hang of it.

# Why are **blokes** like **horoscopes**?

They always tell you what to do and are usually wrong.

# Why are **blokes** like **bank accounts**?

Without a lot of money, they don't generate much interest.

Why are **blokes** like **lawnmowers**?

If you're not pushing one around, then you're riding it.

Why are **blokes** like **used cars**?

Both are easy to get, cheap and unreliable.

# Why are **blokes** like **chocolate bars**?

They're sweet, smooth and they usually head right for your hips.

Why are **blokes** like **holidays**?

They never seem to last long enough.

?

# Why are **blokes** like **mascara**?

They usually run at the first sign of emotion.

Why are **blokes** like **place-mats**?

They only show up when there's food on the table.

Why are **blokes** like **lava lamps**?

Fun to look at but not all that bright.

# Why are **blokes** like **cement**?

After getting laid, they take a long time to get hard.

Why are **blokes** like **plungers**?

They spend most of their lives in a hardware store or the bathroom.

Why are **blokes** like **blenders**?

You need one but you don't know why.

# Why are **blokes** like **toilets**?

Because they're always either engaged, vacant or full of crap.

# Why are **blokes** like **beer bottles**?

Because they're both empty from the neck up.

Why are **blokes** like **popcorn**?

They satisfy you, but only for a little while.

# Why are **blokes** like **bike helmets**?

Handy in an emergency, but otherwise they just look silly.

Why are **blokes** like
**parking spaces?**

Because the good ones are
always gone and the only ones
left are disabled.

# Why are **blokes** like **coffee**?

The best ones are rich, warm and can keep you up all night long.

Why are **blokes** like **spray paint**?

One squeeze and they're all over you.

Why are **blokes** like **cashpoint machines**?

Once they withdraw they lose interest.

Why are **blokes** like **caravans**?

Because they follow wherever you take them.

Why are **blokes** like **laxatives**?

The both irritate the shit out of you.

Why are **blokes** like **sperm**?

They both have only a one in a million chance of becoming a human being.

# Why are **blokes** like **computers**?

You never know how much they mean to you until they go down on you.

# Why are **blokes** like **snowstorms**?

'Cos you don't know when they're coming, how long they're going to last or how many inches you'll get.

Why are **blokes** like **department stores**?

Their clothes should always be half off.

# Why are **blokes** like **dog poos**?

The older they get, the easier they are to pick up.

## Why are **blokes** like **clouds**?

Eventually they bugger off and it's a really nice day.

How can you tell the **difference** between blokes' **real gifts** and their **guilt gifts**?

Guilt gifts are nicer.

**How many** blokes does it take to change a **toilet roll**?

Who knows?
It hasn't happened yet.

?? ?

# How are **blokes** like **noodles**?

They're always in hot water, they lack taste and they need dough.

How can you keep
a **bloke happy**?

Who cares?

How do you **drown** a **muscle man**?

You put a mirror in a pool.

How many blokes does it take to **screw** in a **lightbulb**?

One… men will screw anything.

# How come blokes have such **small balls**?

Because so very few of them can dance.

## How do you **stop** a bloke from **drowning**?

Take your foot off his head.

**How** do you get a bloke to do **sit-ups**?

Put the remote control between his toes.

# How can you tell if a bloke is **well hung**?

You can't get your finger between the rope and his neck.

How do you know when a bloke is gonna say something **clever**?

He starts off with 'My girlfriend says…'

**How many** blokes does it take to change a **lightbulb**?

Three. One to change it and two to listen while he brags about how he screwed it.

## How do you know when your bloke is **getting old**?

When he starts having dry dreams and wet farts.

How many blokes does it take to change a **lightbulb**?

One. He just holds it and waits for the world to revolve around him.

# How does a bloke take a **bubble bath**?

He eats beans for dinner.

## How does a bloke's **mind work**?

It doesn't... it's always on sick leave.

How do you **know** when a bloke is **lying**?

His lips move.

How is a **bloke** like the **weather**?

Nothing can be done to change either one of them.

# How can you tell if a bloke is **excited**?

He's breathing.

## How can you **grow** your own **dope**?

Bury a bloke and wait till spring.

How does a bloke get **air** to his **brain**?

He opens his flies.

# How many blokes does it take to **pop popcorn**?

Three. One to hold the pan and two others to show off and shake the stove.

How does a bloke keep
a woman **screaming**
after **climax**?

He wipes his willy on the curtains.

# How can you find a **committed** bloke?

Look in a mental institution.

How many **divorced blokes** does it take to change a **lightbulb**?

Nobody knows – they never get the house!

How do blokes extend the **washing life** of their **boxer shorts**?

They turn them inside out.

How should you reply to a bloke who says, 'Hey, you're **just my type**'?

'I think you must be mistaken – I have a pulse.'

How do you stop a
**lust-filled bloke**?

Marry him.

How can a bloke tell
when a woman has had
a **good orgasm**?

When the buzzing of her
vibrator stops.

How can you spot the blokes who've **stolen** a job lot of **Viagra**?

They're a bunch of hardened criminals in possession of swollen goods.

How do you know if
a bloke's been in
your **garden**?

Your bins have been knocked
over and your dog is pregnant.

# How do blokes **exercise** on the **beach**?

By sucking in their stomach every time a bikini goes by.